PROCESS AUTOMATION UNLOCKED

TURNING IDEAS INTO IMPACT WITH WINNING BUSINESS CASES

MARIO SMEETS
DÜSSELDORF, GERMANY, 2024

IMPRINT

AUTHOR AND PUBLISHER:
SMEETS INCO UG (HAFTUNGSBESCHRAENKT)
HRB 20286, AMTSGERICHT MOENCHENGLADBACH, GERMANY
MARIO SMEETS
DOHLENWEG 8
41751 VIERSEN, GERMANY

Contents

1. **About the Author and the Book** _____ 7
   2. About the Author _____ 7
   3. Why This Book Matters _____ 8
   4. Who Is This Book for? _____ 9
   5. A note about the content _____ 10
6. **Introduction** _____ 11
   7. Why Estimate ROI? _____ 11
   8. What is Process Automation? _____ 12
9. **Foundations of ROI in Process Automation** _____ 16
   10. Understanding ROI: A Quick Primer _____ 16
   11. The Significance of ROI _____ 17
   12. Typical Mistakes Regarding the ROI _____ 17
       13. Ignoring Unexpected Expenses _____ 17
       14. Exaggerating the Advantages _____ 19
       15. Neglecting to Appreciate Intangibles _____ 20
       16. Underestimating Opposition to Change _____ 20
       17. Only Paying Attention to ROI _____ 21
       18. Ignoring the Time Aspect _____ 22
   19. Last Remark _____ 22
20. **Identifying Automation Opportunities** _____ 23
    21. What qualifies a process ready for automation? _____ 23
    22. Begin with the points of contention _____ 25
    23. Ask appropriate questions _____ 27
    24. Be Alert for Red Flags _____ 28
    25. Manage the Process Pilot-wise _____ 28
    26. Example: Automating a Sales Team's CRM Updates _____ 29
    27. The Reality at Last _____ 30
28. **Building the Business Case** _____ 31
    29. Cost Estimation for Process Automation Projects _____ 31
        30. Dissecting the Expenses _____ 31

	31	How to Clearly Identify the Expenses	35
	32	Typical Cost Estimation Pitfalls	36
	33	The Bottom Line	37

34 Quantifying Benefits of Automation — 38

	35	Straight Benefits: The Simple Wins	38
	36	Deep-Dive into Measurement of Time Savings and Labor Costs	39
	37	The Undiscovered Treasures: Indirect Benefits	43
	38	Strategic Benefits: The Long Run	44
	39	How to Offer Dollar-Value Benefits	45
	40	Typical Mistakes Made in Benefit Calculations	46
	41	How Everything Harmonizes	46

42 Assessing Risk and Uncertainty — 48

	43	Technical Risks: Will the Tech Perform as Anticipated?	48
	44	Operational risks: Will people use it correctly?	49
	45	Financial Risks: Will it stay on budget and provide ROI?	50
	46	Strategic Risks: Will They Match Objectives Over Long Term?	51
	47	Dealing with Uncertainty: What You Don't Know (Yet)	52
	48	Presenting Risk and Uncertainty to Stakeholders	52
	49	The Bottom Line	53

50 *ROI Calculation and Presentation* — 54

51 Framework for Calculation of ROI — 54

	52	First Step: determining expenses	55
	53	Second Step: calculating advantages	56
	54	Third Step: Factor in Time	57
	55	Fourth Step: Conduct a sensitivity analysis	58
	56	Fifth Step: Present the Numbers Clearly	59
	57	An Illustration in Action	59
	58	The Final Thought	60

59 Making a Strong Business Case — 61

	60	Start with the Why: Clearly define the Problem	61
	61	The Solution: Position Automation as Fix	62
	62	Count the advantages and make the value very clear	62
	63	Talk about the risks; be honest	63
	64	Share a Story: Link the Dots	64
	65	Customize the Message by Understanding Your Audience	65
	66	Finish with a call-to-action directive	65
	67	The Bottom Line	66

68 Presenting ROI to Stakeholders — 67

69 *Practical Case Studies and Insights* — 69

70 Case Studies of Successful Automation Projects — 69

	71	Why Should Case Studies Count?	69

	72	Presenting Case Studies: Effective Approach	70
	73	Case Study 1: processing invoices automatically in a SMC	71
	74	Case Study 2: AI Chatbots in Consumer Service for Retailers	72
	75	Case Study 3: Financial Services Automating Compliance Reporting	73
	76	Combining All the Components	74
77		**Industry-Specific ROI Insights**	**75**
	78	From Reactive to Predictive Manufacturing	75
	79	Healthcare: Reducing the Administrative Workload	76
	80	Financial Services: Compliance and Beyond	77
	81	Retail: Improving Consumer Experience	78
	82	Small and Medium Businesses (SMBs): Stretching Resources	78
	83	The Big Picture: Emphasize What Matters Most	79
84		***Bringing It All Together***	**80**
	85	**ROI as the Strategic Lens**	80
	86	**From Statistics to Action**	81
	87	**Anticipating Change**	81
	88	**The Broad Effects of Automation**	82
	89	**A Call to Action**	82
90		***The Road Ahead***	**84**
91		***App.: Key Learnings of the Book in a Nutshell***	**87**
92		***App.: Resources for Estimating and Maximizing ROI***	**88**
	93	**ROI Calculation Frameworks**	88
	94	**Automation Suitability Frameworks**	90
	95	**Risk Assessment Models**	91
	96	**Implementation and Scalability Frameworks**	92
	97	**How These Frameworks Work Together**	93

Figure 1: Automation Suitability Matrix	25
Figure 2: Types of Expenses	32
Figure 3: Example of a Cost Distribution	35
Figure 4: ROI and Payback Period of Automation Projects	58

1   About the Author and the Book

2   About the Author

My name is Mario Smeets, and I've spent the previous 15 years navigating the ever-changing worlds of banking, consulting, and leadership. I am currently the managing director of a consulting firm specializing in process excellence and automation based in Düsseldorf, Germany. My whole career has revolved around one guiding principle:

Helping businesses optimize their operations, streamline workflows, and achieve long-term growth through smart, scalable solutions.

As a process management expert, I've had the opportunity to guide firms of all sizes, from multinational banks to ambitious mid-sized businesses, through the complexities of operational challenges and technological transformation. Over the years, I've seen how the right processes, combined with intelligent automation, can unlock potential, boost efficiencies, and empower teams. However, I've witnessed the frustrations, delays, and complete failures that may occur when automation efforts lack a solid foundation, a clear business case, or effective communication.

This is the purpose for which I wrote this book.

In practice, I've witnessed numerous automation attempts fail due to improper foundation laying, rather than insufficient technology. Too often, ambitious plans fail to deliver results owing to a lack of a compelling business case, a clear understanding of the predicted ROI, or stakeholder agreement. Only meticulous planning, execution, and a robust value measuring strategy can ensure the success of even the most promising technologies. My goal with this book is to address these difficulties head-on and provide a realistic, actionable approach for everyone interested in making automation a success.

3 Why This Book Matters

Automation has become a buzzword in virtually every business. Companies are eager to embrace the future with AI-powered equipment and robotics, expecting that automation will solve their productivity issues. However, the reality is more complex. Automation is not a magical answer; rather, it is a strategic investment that requires meticulous strategy, preparation, and execution. Without a business case that clearly describes the benefits and costs, automation projects can quickly develop into expensive experiments with little to show for their efforts.

This book is crucial because it bridges the gap between aspiration and reality. It's more than just a manual for implementing automation; it's also a toolset for ensuring that automation produces measurable, meaningful outcomes. Whether you're a manager trying to justify an automation program, a team leader seeking to improve operational workflows, or an executive looking for ways to optimize your business, this book contains the answers and tools you need to succeed.

4 Who Is This Book for?

Specialists from a variety of industries who are concerned with process automation are the target audience for this book. Whether you're new to the field or wish to improve your approach, this book offers useful ideas for:

- **Business leaders and executives** must grasp how automation can help them achieve their strategic goals while also improving bottom-line performance.
- **Process Managers and Team Leaders** are responsible for identifying inefficiencies, developing workflows, and implementing operational automation.
- **Consultants and analysts** help businesses evaluate automation potential, and they need credible frameworks for calculating ROI and establishing business cases.
- **Technology enthusiasts and automation professionals** are seeking to go beyond technical implementation and understand the business implications of their work.

The content is intentionally approachable, integrating practical frameworks, real-world observations, and actionable advice. You can apply the principles in this book to your specific challenges whether you work in banking, manufacturing, healthcare, retail, or any other industry.

5 A note about the content

This book's information and examples are based on two main sources: real-world experience and illustrated examples designed to clarify complex ideas. I've anonymized many of the case studies, which are based on genuine projects I've worked on to preserve privacy. In some cases, I've altered or created conditions to better show specific themes or difficulties. The inclusion of authentic and personalized examples ensures that the teachings are both practical and widely applicable.

I hope this book not only provides you with the tools you need to succeed but also inspires you to think critically about how automation may benefit your organization. Let us work together to close the gap between ambition and execution, translating ideas into long-term outcomes.

If you like this book, I would be very happy about a positive evaluation. This will help other readers to decide whether the book is something for them.

And if you have any suggestions or questions, please email me at **info@mario-smeets.de**. *Happy to hear from you.*

6 Introduction

7 Why Estimate ROI?

Every business leader wants to know one thing before greenlighting a project: *Is the project worth the investment?*

When it comes to process automation, the stakes are even higher. It's not just about saving money; it's about proving that the automation initiative will deliver tangible, measurable results. But here's the problem: ROI isn't always easy to pin down for automation projects. Sure, you can calculate basic cost savings from reduced labor or faster processing times. But what about the harder-to-quantify benefits? Improved customer satisfaction, fewer errors, or the long-term scalability that automation can bring? These are real gains, but they can feel like a guessing game if you don't have a solid framework and even the supposedly simple cost savings-based business cases are difficult to implement in practice, especially when it comes to determining which costs should be applied, how and when, and what the real savings are.

That's where this book comes in. It's not about drowning you in financial jargon or overwhelming spreadsheets. It's about giving you a *practical, step-by-step approach* to estimate ROI for process automation projects. By the time you're done, you'll have the tools to confidently present the value of automation to your stakeholders—backed by clear data, compelling arguments, and a plan that works.

Because here's the truth: In today's world, automation isn't just a nice-to-have; it's a must-have. And proving the ROI is how you move it from the "wish list" to the budget.
In today's competitive business environment, every investment must be justified, and process automation is no exception.

Despite its importance, quantifying ROI for automation can be challenging. Automation impacts both tangible metrics, like cost savings, and intangible ones, such as employee satisfaction or customer experience. These intangibles can be difficult to measure and are often overlooked in traditional calculations. Moreover, businesses sometimes struggle to account for hidden costs, such as training or integration with legacy systems, which can skew projections.

This book aims to demystify the ROI estimation process for process automation projects. By breaking it into manageable steps, providing actionable tools, and exploring real-world examples, you'll be equipped to present a compelling case for automation and ensure your organization's investments deliver measurable value.

8 What is Process Automation?

Process automation is not just a buzzword in today's business vocabulary, but a transformative tool that is changing how companies run. Fundamentally, process automation is the application of technology to carry out rule-based, repetitious operations historically done by humans. It's about simplifying processes, raising accuracy, and relieving staff members from boring tasks so they could concentrate on more important work. To really know what process automation is, though, we must go beyond its definition and investigate its influence, development, and underlying ideas that support its success.

Imagine a finance department in which staff members manually enter data from invoices into a system, cross-check numbers, and email approvals back and forth for hours every day. Despite their necessity, these tasks rarely inspire me. They are time-consuming, repetitious, and prone to mistakes. Imagine now a system that automatically gathers data from bills, checks the information against purchase orders, and forwards disparities to the relevant person for inspection. The work spans minutes rather than hours. Process automation, which involves the flawless integration of technology into systems to enhance their speed, reliability, and efficiency, is currently underway.

Process automation has beauty in its universality. Process automation is applicable almost everywhere in business and industry, from customer service and HR to production and logistics. The common thread is that it focuses on procedures that involve predictable, repetitive actions. These could range from creating monthly reports to inventory control or new staff onboarding. Automation can intervene to precisely and quickly perform tasks that follow a clear set of guidelines anywhere there is one.

Still, automation is about change rather than only efficiency. Routine chores, when automated, not only expedite their completion but also enhance their quality. Oversight or tiredness causes no errors. Once dependent on email threads or spreadsheets, processes now centralize and become transparent. Teams who felt mired in administrative tasks are free to concentrate on strategic goals, creativity, and problem-solving. Automation fundamentally alters how companies run and lets them accomplish more with less.

It's important to understand the distinctions between process automation and its limitations. Neither is it about substituting machines for people nor is it a one-size-fits-all fix. Rather, it is about teamwork—using technology to augment human capacity. For instance, robots screening resumes do not replace an HR manager, freeing her to concentrate on assessing outstanding prospects and building corporate culture. Automation improves human input by handling repetitive labor; it does not replace it. There are several kinds of process automation, each appropriate for a distinct degree of organizational requirement and complexity. At the simpler end of the scale, there is basic task automation—that is, putting up systems that automatically email reminders or responses. More advanced robotic process automation (RPA) replicates human operations, including data extraction, application login, and computation using software bots. Intelligent automation thus integrates artificial intelligence (AI) with RPA to handle activities requiring some degree of reasoning, such as trend analysis of consumer behavior or data interpretation without structure.

The scalability of process automation makes it so potent. Starting small by automating one chore or workflow, you can grow incrementally as you observe outcomes. Beginning with its financial department, a corporation may subsequently expand to automate customer inquiries, inventory control, and other related areas. Every action builds on the next to produce a cascade of creativity and effectiveness throughout the company.
Even with its promise, process automation is about people and procedures, not technology. To achieve success, we must use automation deliberately and with a clear understanding of the workflow it aims to enhance. Automation alone cannot transform a poorly designed process into an effective one. Therefore, its effectiveness depends critically on a thorough study of the present processes, a dedication to ongoing development, and the active participation of the teams impacted by automation.

Process automation has developed from a competitive advantage to a need in the hectic corporate climate of today. Companies that welcome automation are positioning themselves to be more nimble, resilient, and creative, not only increasing efficiency. Automation marks the beginning of a new way of working where technology and human ingenuity combine to accomplish more than ever before, not the conclusion of the tale.

Fundamentally, process automation is about generating space—space for companies to create, space for workers to flourish, and space for organizations to concentrate on what really counts. It is a technique for releasing potential rather than only a means of simplifying processes. The potential of automation is only beginning to unfold as we continue to integrate smarter technologies into our processes.

This is why knowing how to calculate ROI is so important. It gives you a way to quantify the benefits and justify the investment. It separates flashy buzzwords from the real-world impact. Most importantly, it ensures you're automating the right things for the right reasons.

In the chapters ahead, we'll walk through how to spot automation opportunities, calculate the costs, estimate the benefits, and build a business case that gets people on board. By the end of this book, you won't just understand ROI—you'll be able to prove it. Let's get started.

9 Foundations of ROI in Process Automation

10 Understanding ROI: A Quick Primer

Let's start with the basics: *What is ROI?* It's a straightforward question with a deceptively simple answer: ROI, or Return on Investment, is the financial yardstick that tells you whether something is worth your time and money. At its core, the formula looks like this:

$$ROI(\%) = \left(\frac{Net\ Benefits}{Total\ Costs}\right) * 100$$

Net benefits? That's the money saved or earned because of your project. Total costs? That's every dollar you spent to make it happen. Multiply it by 100, and voilà—you've got your ROI percentage.

Let's avoid oversimplifying, though. ROI calculations for automation initiatives are rarely that straightforward. Determining the actual costs and advantages of automation can be daunting since it affects so many areas of a company, including operations, IT, compliance, and even human resources. Step-by-step dissection is crucial.

1. The first of the three pillars of return on investment is costs, which include hardware, software licenses, implementation fees, and maintenance. If you miss one, your return on investment will appear higher on paper than it does in practice.
2. Advantages: Consider financial savings from fewer human mistakes, quicker processing, or shorter workdays. Don't stop there, though. Consider the indirect advantages as well, such as improved customer satisfaction or happier staff.

3. Time: ROI is about when you get it, not simply what you get. The sooner you get your money back, the better.

11   The Significance of ROI

ROI is your argument, not simply a figure. It's how you persuade your boss that this project should be at the top of the list or get the CFO to approve of that shiny new automation tool. It also has to do with how you handle expectations. A reliable ROI estimate guarantees that nobody is taken by surprise when the real results are revealed. Furthermore, automation projects may appear to be fancy solutions to look for a problem if they don't have a return on investment. The last thing you want is that.

12   Typical Mistakes Regarding the ROI

If you're not attentive, the ROI calculation for process automation can quickly get complicated. If it fails in the real world, a fantastic ROI on paper is meaningless. Let's examine some of the most typical mistakes that can throw off your calculations and, more crucially, how to avoid them.

13   Ignoring Unexpected Expenses

The issue:
The true cost of automation is easy to underestimate. The cost of the program and possibly the cost of hiring a consultant will be covered, of course, but what about all the minor extras? Reconfiguring outdated workflows, training your staff, and implementation downtime can quickly mount up. All of a sudden, your "low-cost" project is depleting your finances like a ravenous kid at a buffet.

The Solution:
Consider expenses in layers. Software, implementation, and maintenance are the most evident. Next, delve further:

- The cost of integration: How much time and money will it take to integrate your current tools with the new system? Legacy systems have a reputation for being unpredictable.
- Training Expenses: Will the new system require training for your team to use? Don't count on it to "click."
- Downtime Costs: How much productivity is lost during setup? The cost of even a few days of disruption can be high.
- The Costs of Scaling: Will the system expand to meet your needs, or will you eventually have to pay extra for more users or features?

One sometimes overlooked fact is that the more automated a system is, the more dependent it is on system-specific updates, releases, and fixes. Errors and failures may arise if things are not planned for and tested, ideally with regression tests: hidden expenses. However, even if pre-planning is done, the expense of the pre-planning and analysis is borne by the employees who must be on hand to test, inspect, and, if needed, modify the bots. Therefore, include a buffer in your estimations. Be prepared for the unexpected by assuming it will occur.

14   Exaggerating the Advantages

<u>The issue:</u>
Automation holds out the thrilling promise of quicker workflows, fewer mistakes, and more contented workers. Here's the catch, though: believing that these advantages would appear completely, without any problems, and overnight. Benefits in the real world are frequently less immediate and smaller than anticipated. Consider this instance: You think you'll save 20 hours a week by automating a process. That sounds fantastic, doesn't it? However, what happens if workers waste the time they have freed up or if the automation only completes a portion of the task? Suddenly, both your ROI and your time savings decrease.

<u>The Solution:</u>
When making estimates, exercise caution. Consider this:

- What is practical? Make moderate assumptions at first on efficiency benefits. Calculate ROI based on 10 hours if you believe automation will save 20 hours. It's a win if it works out better.
- What is the curve of adoption? The new system won't be quickly adopted by everyone. Take resistance to change or a learning curve into account.
- What is the value of partial automation? Adjust your savings if the procedure isn't entirely automated. For instance, just count savings for the 70% of the workload that is handled by automation.

Before expressing your assumptions, test them. Delivering more while making fewer promises is preferable to the opposite.

15   Neglecting to Appreciate Intangibles

The issue:
The issue is that not all of the benefits of automation can be quantified. How can a smoother customer experience or happier staff be quantified? A lot of teams just exclude these, thus their ROI estimates don't provide the whole picture.

The Solution:
- Look for a proxy if you are unable to measure it directly. For instance: Examine retention rates to gauge employee morale. Longer employee retention saves you money on hiring and training new staff.
- Client Contentment: Make use of analytics such as customer turnover rates or Net Promoter Score (NPS). Determine the impact on revenue of retaining those customers if automation lowers turnover by 5%.
- Error Reduction: Calculate how much it will cost to correct errors, including lost profits, fines from the government, and wasted time.

Recognizing these advantages improves your argument, even if they are more difficult to define. Don't go overboard, though; intangible advantages should supplement real data rather than take its place.

16   Underestimating Opposition to Change

The issue:
The problem with automation is that people don't necessarily enjoy it. Resistance can impede adoption and reduce your return on investment, whether it's due to a fear of losing their job or simply inertia. If no one wants to use a sophisticated new tool, what good is it?

The Solution:
- Include change management as part of your strategy: Early employee involvement is key. To give people a sense of ownership over the solution, let them assist in identifying which processes should be automated.
- Communicate intelligibly. Instead of replacing them, present automation as a tool to help them do their tasks more easily.
- Offer assistance. Quick access to troubleshooting, training sessions, and simple-to-follow instructions can make all the difference.

When assessing the benefits, account for a slower rate of adoption. Plan for six months if you believe the team will be at full capacity in three.

17   Only Paying Attention to ROI

The Issue:
Return on investment is more than just money. The ability to extend operations without hiring more staff or more easily fulfill compliance standards are just two examples of the strategic value that automation can provide that isn't necessarily evident in financial numbers. The wider influence may be underestimated if the immediate financial gain is the only thing considered.

The Solution:
Consider more than just the spreadsheet. What is automation worth in the long run? For instance:
- Scalability: To what extent could your company expand without hiring more employees?
- Compliance: To what extent can automating regulatory procedures reduce risk?
- Strategic Agility: How does automation allow resources to be allocated to more important or creative tasks?

Incorporate these into your ROI presentation as qualitative points. Even though they don't have a monetary value, they frequently work in your favor.

18 Ignoring the Time Aspect

The issue:
Although it can be forgotten in the enthusiasm, ROI doesn't happen overnight. When stakeholders don't receive the results they're hoping for, their trust in the project may be damaged. There will be disappointment if the ROI realization timeline is not communicated.

The Solution:
Have reasonable expectations:
- When calculating ROI, factor in a payback period. How much time will it take to get the money back? Use this as a benchmark to gauge your progress.
- Display a benefits timeline. For instance, whereas staff productivity increases may take six months while they get used to the new system, mistake reduction may start right away.
- Emphasize early victories. Building momentum can be aided by even modest accomplishments, such as automating a single step in a broader workflow.

19 Last Remark

Getting the numbers correct is only one aspect of ROI estimation; another is developing a successful strategy. By avoiding these mistakes, you increase the accuracy of your calculations and increase the likelihood that your automation project will be successful overall. ROI is the tactic that makes automation work, but automation itself is a tool.

20 Identifying Automation Opportunities

Regarding automation, half the fight is choosing the correct procedures to start first. Start with the incorrect ones, and before you have shown any value you will burn through your budget and goodwill. But make sensible decisions and your showcase project will have rapid victories, momentum building, and questions from your stakeholders about, "What else can we automate?"
Let us explore how to spot those great prospects.

21 What qualifies a process ready for automation?

Not every process exists equally. At least for now, some are better left in human hands; others are ideal candidates for automation. The ideal automated systems usually include a few main traits:

- **Repetitive**: There is little variety in the method used every time. Consider chores including payroll computations, invoice processing, or data entry.
- **Rule-Based**: The process operates within well-defined guidelines. "If the invoice total exceeds $10,000, route it to the manager for approval," says one. Automation may suffer if people are making decisions or exceptions at every stage of the process.
- **High Volume**: Because the time savings compound rapidly, daily, weekly, or hundreds of times a month processes that happen often offer the best return on investment.

- **Error-prone**: Tasks high in human mistake risk, such as regulatory reporting or manual data entry, would much benefit from the precision of automation.
- **Time-Consuming**: Automating a procedure that takes hours or days will free a lot of time.

When it comes to identifying the two most useful dimensions, it is certainly process complexity and process volume. Figure 1 relates these two dimensions to each other. Process complexity is plotted on the x-axis. It varies from low to high. The process volume is plotted on the y axis. It also varies from low to high. The upper left quadrant contains processes that have a high priority for automation. They have a high level of process volume and low complexity, meaning they are easy to automate. Processes with only a low process volume and low complexity can still be automated or can be considered for automation. The same applies to processes with high volumes, but which are very complex. The lower right quadrant contains processes that are generally not suitable for automation or only suitable for automation with priority B. This is always the case if the processes only have low volumes and are highly complex.

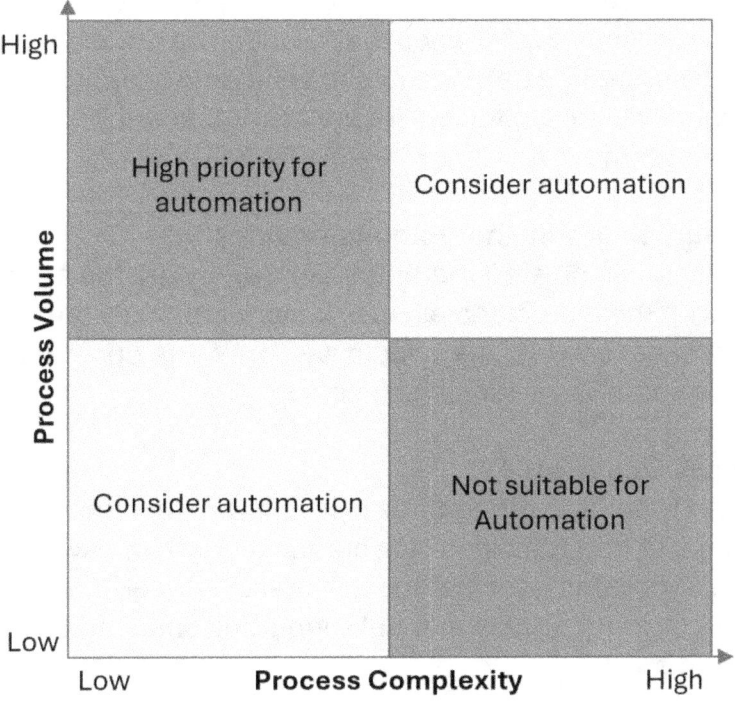

Figure 1: Automation Suitability Matrix

Consider the accounts payable (AP) staff of a corporation. They manually handle 1,000 bills every month, which requires data entry, cross-checks against purchase orders, and management approval seeking. It's repetitious, rule-based, high-volume, error-prone, time-consuming—a perfect storm of automation possibility.

22 Begin with the points of contention

Starting with your main bottlenecks will help you the best. These are the procedures slowing down your company, annoying your staff, or preventing expansion. Questions yourself:

What's eating up time?
See where most of your staff spends their working day. Are their records kept in spreadsheets? Chained to send emails approving decisions? Handily filling up forms? These are outstanding candidates for automation.

From what sources are the complaints arising?
See your supervisors and staff members. Since they are the ones daily dealing with the inefficiencies, they know where they are. "This process takes forever," they would say, or "We're constantly fixing mistakes here." These are gold insights.

Why Are Delays Occurring?
Delays frequently point to procedures including too many redundant steps or handoffs involving human labor. You have uncovered an opportunity, for instance, if it takes a week to onboard a new hire since HR is manually inputting data into three separate systems.

Chart the Path.
You should map a possible automation target once you have one in mind. This isn't sophisticated; a basic flowchart or step-by-step sketch will suffice. The objective is to grasp:

- The beginning of the procedure.
- The personal actions involved.
- Points of decisions when guidelines apply.
- For every stage, who—or what—is in charge?
- The process finishes in what way?

As a matter of fact, your map for the AP process might resemble this:
- Get a bill.
- Set it against a purchase order.
- Enter it into the ERP system if the sums line up.
- Flag it for hand inspection if the quantities differ.

- Send the invoice to the management for approval along route.
- Procedure payment.

By means of mapping the process, you may spot inefficiencies including duplicate processes or manual handoffs and guarantee that nothing is missed while developing your automation solution.

23   Ask appropriate questions

Not every operation merits automation. Review every applicant critically before jumping right in. Ask the following important questions:

- **Is the process stable?**
  Automation excels in clearly defined, unlikely to change processes. Wait until your workflow settles down if it is still changing or contains too many variables.
- **What is the potential ROI?**
  Examine the expenses and advantages. Automation will save how much time and money? With what speed will those savings mount up? If the implementation costs $50,000, a process saving $1,000 a year might not be worth automating.
- **What is the degree of complexity?**
  Your initial project would be perfect for simple procedures since they are faster and less expensive to automate. More complicated procedures may yield more benefits but call either specialized equipment or customizing.
- **Does it fit the objectives of business?**
  Automation is about impact not only in terms of efficiency. Whether it's cost control, customer experience

enhancement, or operational scalability, concentrate on activities supporting the strategic goals of your business.

24 Be Alert for Red Flags

Although automation offers great promise, not every process fits well. Exercise care regarding:

- **Low-Volume Tasks**: Should a procedure only occur a few times a year, automating it could not be worth the expenses.
- **Procedures Demanding Creativity or Judgement**: For present, tasks including brainstorming, bargaining, or proposal writing belong better to people.
- **High Variability**: Automation may find difficulty if the process involves unstructured data (handwritten notes) or changes often.

25 Manage the Process Pilot-wise

Start modestly once you have selected a technique. Before committing to a major deployment, a pilot project allows you test the waters. Here's how you approach it:

- **Describe success**. Give the pilot specific objectives include cutting processing time by half or removing eighty percent of mistakes.
- **Count Results**: Track important indicators such time saved, cost savings, and error rates to see whether the automation provides the anticipated results.

- **Get input**: Talk to those applying the automated system. Are the adjustments satisfying to them? Exact difficulties exist?

26   Example: Automating a Sales Team's CRM Updates

The Issue:
Every week, the sales staff spends hours manually inputting data into the CRM system, updating leads, noting calls, and following development. Less time for real selling results from its repetitious, tiresome nature and tendency toward mistakes.

The solution:
Install a process automation solution that straight into the CRM synzes data from call logs, calendars, and emails. Sales representatives simply have to verify or change the data, therefore reducing their administrative load half-way.

The results:
- Ten hours a week each representative saves time.
- For a team of ten representatives working at $50 per hour, annual cost reductions come to $52,000.
- Enhanced accuracy—no more incomplete records or missed changes.

27 The Reality at Last

Finding the appropriate automation prospects mostly depends on concentration. Start with the processes that cause the most problems; then, search for repetitious, rule-based, high-volume ones. Choose a few high-impact successes to create momentum and demonstrate the value of automation to your team and stakeholders; avoid trying to automate everything at once. Get that correctly, and you will be building the basis for a successful, scalable automation plan.

28 Building the Business Case

29   Cost Estimation for Process Automation Projects

Process automation project cost estimation might be likened to attempting to hit a changing target. On the surface, it's simple to concentrate on the apparent figures: a few servers, software licenses, and possibly a consultant. The problem is that you're only giving half the narrative if you stop there. A combination of up-front fees, recurring obligations, and those elusive hidden costs that often appear when you least expect them to make up the true cost of automation. Your ROI projections will eventually be called into question if you are not diligent in this step.
Let's examine the specifics.

30   Dissecting the Expenses

Consider automation expenses as a three-layered pyramid (Figure 2) initial, recurring, and hidden costs. Although each layer adds complexity, you'll cover all the bases if you approach them methodically.

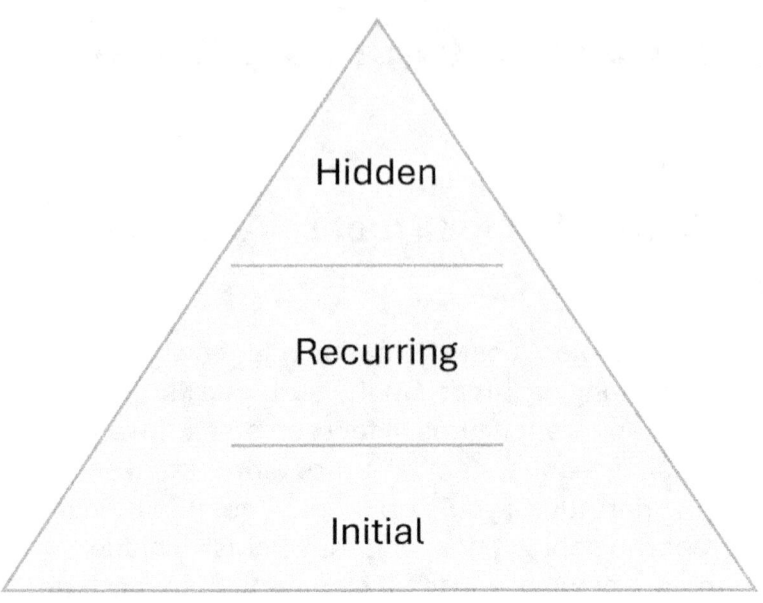

Figure 2: Types of Expenses

Initial or Upfront Expenses: The Expensive Things

Before you even turn on your automation project, you will have to pay these expenses. Although they are typically the simplest to compute, they can also be the most daunting.

- **Software licensing** is frequently the biggest line item, regardless of whether you're utilizing workflow platforms like Zapier or Robotic Process Automation (RPA) products like UiPath. For enterprise-grade solutions, licenses can cost tens of thousands of dollars, while those for individual users can cost a few hundred dollars.
- **Implementation Costs**: Many companies undervalue this. It can be costly and time-consuming to modify automation technologies to match your unique procedures. Consider their fees if you're dealing with a consultant or vendor. For instance, it could take weeks of development to set up an RPA bot to process invoices.

- **Hardware expenses** are determined by the size of your project. The cloud is where many automation solutions operate, reducing the need for hardware. However, if you're using on-premises systems, you may require improved infrastructure or new servers.
- **Process Reengineering**: Automating your current procedures is rarely ideal right out of the box. Workflows will frequently need to be modified to account for the technology. This could involve redistributing internal resources or employing a business analyst to improve your procedures.

Recurring Expenses: The cost of maintaining automated automation is not a one-time expenditure

There are ongoing expenses to maintain the system's functionality after it is put into place.

- **Updates and maintenance**: Software is not self-maintained. You'll require bug patches, updates, and new features over time. While some suppliers charge maintenance separately, others include it in their licensing fees. For instance, 20% of your original licensing money may be required for an annual maintenance contract.
- **Support and Training**: Your staff must be trained in the efficient use of the automation tools. This can entail setting up workshops, creating documentation, or employing trainers. Ongoing assistance may also be necessary for troubleshooting or orienting new hires.
- **Scaling Costs**: Your company's automation requirements will increase as it expands. extra bots, extra licenses, or system integration can be required. If you don't account for scalability in your initial planning, these expenses may surprise you.

Upfront expenses and continuous expenses add up to **"Total Investment Costs"**. These form the numerator of the Payback formula, which - in relation to automation projects - is presented in more detail later.

Hidden Costs: The Unexpected Expenses

This is when things become complex. Although these expenses aren't typically included in the original proposal or vendor estimate, if you're not ready, they could significantly affect your budget.

- **Integration with Legacy Systems**: While automation technologies are fantastic, they must work well with the infrastructure you already have. You may require special development to fill the gap if your systems are out-of-date or do not support APIs. This can easily turn into a significant cost.
- **Downtime During Implementation**: Some aspects of your process may need to be put on hold while you set up the automation. For instance, there may be delays during the switch to the new system if you're automating payroll processing. Productivity losses during this time can mount up.
- **Opportunity Costs**: Since automation projects demand your team's time and focus, other projects may suffer delays. It's critical to take into consideration both the resources you're reallocating and the possible value they could have produced in other places.
- **Vendor Lock-In**: Changing vendors later on could be expensive if you go with a proprietary solution. The bill may increase due to retraining staff, data transfer expenses, and migration fees.

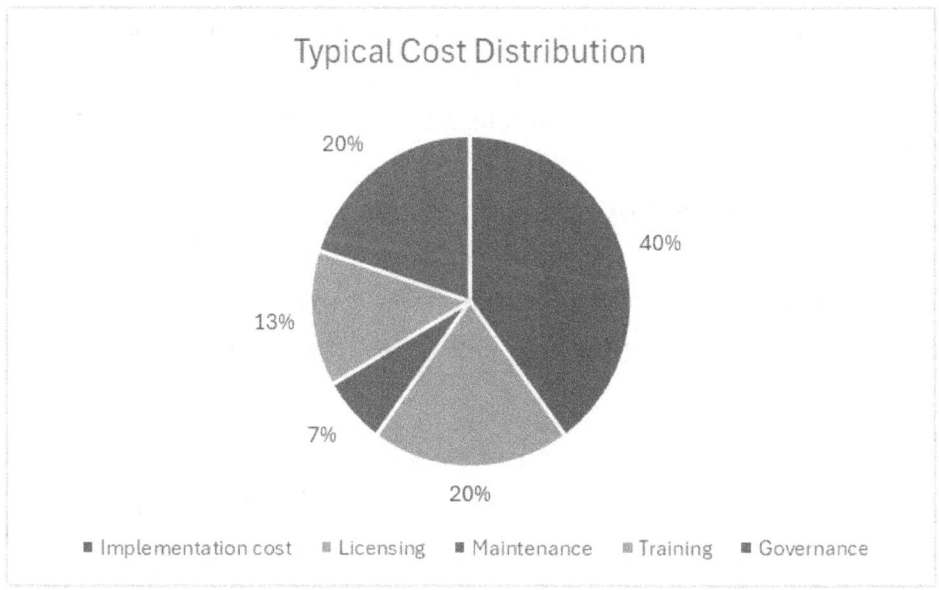

Figure 3: Example of a Cost Distribution

Figure 3 shows an example of a typical cost distribution of automation projects.

31 How to Clearly Identify the Expenses

How do you put everything together now that you know what to look for? Granularity is crucial. Provide as much information as you can on costs; don't leave anything up to speculation. Here's how:

- **Obtain Quotes in Advance**: Request comprehensive proposals from vendors. Request an explanation of the costs associated with implementation, licensing, and support. It will be simpler to create your budget if it is more detailed.
- **Speak with Your IT Staff**: Your IT staff can assist you in determining hardware requirements, integration difficulties, and other technical expenses you might overlook. Include them early in the conversation.

- **Utilize Historical Data**: Use the figures from previous projects that your business has undertaken that are comparable to this one as a starting point. They can help you anticipate things.
- **Create a buffer** since unforeseen events happen no matter how carefully you prepare. Set aside 10–20% of your budget for unforeseen expenses. If expenses surpass your expectations, this will allow you some leeway.

32 Typical Cost Estimation Pitfalls

When estimating expenditures, it's simple to make a mistake, even with the best of intentions. The following errors should be avoided:

- **Underestimating Complexity**: Although automation may appear straightforward at first, it becomes increasingly intricate as you go deeper. Processes frequently require more permissions, systems, or procedures than you first think.
- **Ignoring Long-Term Costs**: A lot of companies concentrate so much on up-front expenditure that they neglect ongoing costs. Recall that years, not months, are used in the ROI calculation.
- **Ignoring Scale**: What would happen if your automation project became extremely successful? Can a larger workload be supported by your infrastructure? Your cost study should include scalability from the start.
- **Ignoring Non-Financial Costs**: In terms of productivity and morale, employee resistance, training weariness, or interruptions to current workflows can also "cost" your

company money. Even if these aren't usually measurable, you should nevertheless take them into account.

33   The Bottom Line

Although cost estimating isn't very attractive, it serves as the basis for your ROI computation and, eventually, your business case. If you make a mistake with this, everything else breaks down. Investigate all three levels of the pyramid: initial, recurring, and hidden expenses. Be realistic, thorough, and ready for everything. Automation can yield amazing benefits, but only if you approach it with an open mind. You'll position yourself for a project that is both economical and efficient if you can master the cost estimation procedure.

34 Quantifying Benefits of Automation

Estimating costs is about knowing what you're paying; quantifying benefits is about proving what you're getting. To be clear, showing outstanding statistics to your stakeholders is only one aspect of success. It entails persuasively arguing for why automaton is the best course of action. There are direct, indirect, even strategic advantages; proving the real return on your investment calls for knowing how to measure them. Let us split it.

35 Straight Benefits: The Simple Wins

Usually, the first things that come to me are the easiest to measure. They often lead to time and money savings; hence they are easily related to your bottom line. Here's how to measure them:

- **Time Savings**: Since automation thrives on repetitious labor, the clearest benefit is often the time savings it offers. To put this into numerical form, find out how long a process now takes, how often it occurs, and how much time automation may save. Double that then by the workers' hourly pay for the task.
  Example: For 10 hours every week, your HR department, for example, personally onboards new employees. With automation, that process runs two hours a week. At $30 per hour for the HR team, you are saving $240 every week—more than $12,000 yearly.
- **Error reduction**: People make mistakes, so error reduction is important. Errors cost money, whether they are corrected for a spelling mistake in an invoice, a customer order or a compliance penalty. Reducing mistakes clearly has economic advantages.
  Example: 5% of the bills generated by your manual data

entry system show mistakes that cause yearly fines and rework totaling $50,000. Should 90% of those errors be eliminated, automation may save $45,000 annually.

- **Increased Output**: Faster procedures mean more work done in the same amount of time. This is especially beneficial for companies that deal with consumers since speed usually translates into better consumer experiences.

Example: Automating customer service, for example, lets your employees answer 20% more queries each hour. Ten thousand questions a month and each one generates $10, thus you have an extra $20,000 every month.

36   Deep-Dive into Measurement of Time Savings and Labor Costs

Time savings and lower personnel costs are two of the most obvious and quantifiable advantages you can draw on when crafting a strong case for automation. These advantages appeal to the finance team as well as others throughout the company since they immediately affect output, efficiency, and employee satisfaction. Measuring these advantages precisely, though, calls for a rigorous methodology. Said another way, "We'll save time and money" is insufficient. Based on actual data, reasonable assumptions, and a strong knowledge of your present procedures, you must precisely measure exactly how much time and money.

Start with the baseline: knowing present efforts.
You must have a thorough awareness of the present before you can evaluate time savings or lowered labor costs. This entails charting the process you wish to automate and timing today's completion of it. Here, a process map or workflow diagram could prove to be a highly useful tool. Starting with every stage of the present workflow—receiving invoices, data entry, validation, approvals, and archiving—you can then automate invoice processing. Decide who is in charge of every chore, how long it usually takes, and how often it happens.

Accurate timing of these tasks is vital. You might start by asking staff members to log their process time over a representative period, say one or two weeks, or by watching them. Employees who report an average of 10 minutes per invoice and handle 1,000 invoices per month collectively spend 10,000 minutes, or approximately 167 hours, on invoice processing each month. Calculation of time savings starts with this baseline.

Finding Automatable and Repetitive Tasks
Every chore in a workflow won't be a candidate for automation. Emphasize regular, rule-based chores that call for little to no human judgment. For automation in our invoice processing example, jobs like matching invoices to purchase orders or inserting invoice data into an ERP system are usually best. Conversely, jobs requiring sophisticated judgment—such as settling conflicts with suppliers—may still call for human supervision.

After noting the automated chores, find out what proportion of the whole workflow they account for. Automation has the potential to reduce process time by up to seventy percent, as data entry and validation account for seventy percent of the overall invoice processing time.

Time Saving Estimation

Automation speeds up repetitive tasks rather than merely cutting down on their duration. Far faster than a human, a bot or script can handle bills in seconds. Determine the time savings by comparing the anticipated duration of each job after automation with the actual time required for each task. As a matter of fact:

- Currently, each invoice's data entry takes five minutes.
- The post-automation estimated data input time is thirty seconds.

This improvement saves 4,500 minutes, or 75 hours, every month by cutting total data entry time from 5,000 minutes to 500 minutes for 1,000 invoices each month. To get a whole picture of overall time saved, multiply this by the number of staff members doing the work.

Turning Time Savings into Monetary Value

Time savings are significant, but if you want to determine ROIs, you must translate them into monetary value. This involves calculating the total cost of the personnel performing the work. Salary, perks, and other costs like office space and equipment comprise fully loaded expenses. If the typical fully loaded hourly cost of your accounts payable staff is $30, for instance, the 75 hours saved on data input equal $2,250 in monthly savings, or $27,000 yearly.

Handling partial time reallocation in accounting

Time saved may not always convert exactly into lower labor costs. If automation saves 10 hours per month for a full-time employee, it may not result in a reduction in headcount, but rather in the transfer of time to more valuable tasks. This is a crucial distinction to make when presenting your business case. Indicate clearly whether time savings would lead to lower labor costs, such as reducing overtime or outsourcing, or higher production, such as allowing staff members to handle more invoices or emphasizing strategic objectives.

For example, the value resides in higher capacity rather than immediate cost savings if automation lets a customer care team answer 50% more questions without adding more workers. You can estimate the opportunity cost of not automating—what you would pay for extra hires to increase capacity—and use that as a proxy for labor cost reductions.

Calculating Indirect Reductions and Ripple Effects

Reductions in labor costs and time savings often have knock-on consequences outside of the local operation. As a matter of fact:

- Automation greatly lowers the possibility of human mistakes, so saving the time and money required in error correction. Automation's accuracy might save an additional 200 minutes per month if 10% of manually entered invoices include mistakes needing an average of 20 minutes to fix.
- Employees released from repetitive activities generally show greater job satisfaction, which can help to lower turnover and the related training and hiring expenses.
- Faster Cycle Times: As demonstrated in accounts receivable automation, or customer happiness via customer service chatbots, shortening the time needed to finish a transaction can improve cash flow.

Your company case should contain these indirect benefits even if their quantification is more difficult. A 20% increase in staff retention, for instance, might save $10,000 yearly on hiring expenses.

Monitoring Post-Implementation Data
Tracking real results against your expectations is crucial once automation is underway. You can also track process time using built-in analytics from your automation platform or time-tracking solutions. Check this information against your baseline to confirm the time savings and, should necessary, modify your ROI computation. Ask staff members also how the automation has affected their job satisfaction and workloads.

Through regular evaluation and analysis of these findings, you not only demonstrate the worth of your present automation project but also get knowledge to follow-up projects. This iterative method creates a culture of ongoing improvement over time, therefore guaranteeing that your efforts on automation yield long-lasting advantages.

37   The Undiscovered Treasures: Indirect Benefits

Though more difficult to measure, these benefits are also rather important. They improve the general state of your business even if they do not show up as a line item on a financial report.

- **Employee satisfaction** is never derived from mind-numbing, repeated tasks. Automating these allows your staff to focus on other critical responsibilities, hence improving morale and reducing attrition. High turnover is expensive; replacement of an employee can cost anywhere from 50% to 200% of their annual salary when you consider recruiting, onboarding, and delayed production. For instance, an automated onerous reporting system lowers turnover by 10% and raises the engagement scores for your team. If turnover were costing you $200,000 a year, you could save $20,000.

- **Faster response times**, **less errors**, and **more consistent service** help happy customers to be. Contented consumers stay longer and spend more money. Automating order tracking, for example, lowers customer complaints by thirty percent, therefore enhancing retention rates. You will have earned an extra $50,000 if you retain 50 more clients and one is worth $1,000 a year.
- **Compliance and Risk Reduction**: Automated processes are easier to audit and less likely to incorporate human error, so one runs less risk of penalties or reputation damage. Companies in regulated sectors know that this advantage might be rather significant even if it is challenging to project the cost of something that never happens.

38   Strategic Benefits: The Long Run

These benefits prepare your company for long-term success even if they do not immediately pay off an investment. Think of them as future competitiveness, agility, and scalability investments.

- **Scalability**: Hiring more workers is the only way manual procedures might expand without increasing costs. Since automation scales without resulting in a proportional increase in expenses, it helps you to monitor growth more precisely. For instance, you would have to staff three more people to handle a 20% rise in orders without automation. At $50,000 apiece, automation saves $150,000 annually.

- **Agility**: Automated processes are easier to adjust when company needs to evolve. This flexibility could transform fast developing industries. For instance, automation efficiently manages an unexpected surge in customer support demand during a new release, therefore saving wasted money and improving your company's standing.
- **Innovation**: Automation releases resources so your team may focus on important initiatives such market development and product introductions.

39   How to Offer Dollar-Value Benefits

Giving monetary value to many benefits feels arbitrary, especially in relation to strategic and indirect ones. These techniques help to give it more substance:

- Use benchmarks to evaluate the impact of automation; refer to case studies or industry standards. Studies show, for example, that automating customer service typically saves thirty percent of the cost.
- Use your own data to project savings from historical performance. Start with, say, a 20% drop in error rates from past automation initiatives.
- Work backwards: After considering the probable impact—more retention rates, for example—determine the financial outcome (retained consumers = more revenue).
- Stakeholders prefer realistic thinking; be conservative. If you are not sure the degree of the advantage, err on the side of caution. Overdelivering and under-promising is usually preferable than the reverse.

40 Typical Mistakes Made in Benefit Calculations

Even the best-intentioned study can go wrong. Stay clear of the following traps:

- **Double Counting**: Take great care not to give more than one source the same advantage. Higher output and time savings, for example, are usually connected; listing them as separate benefits will distort your numbers.
- **Ignoring Intangibles**: Something isn't inherently less valuable just because it's hard to measure. Be honest about intangible benefits like staff morale and weave them into your narrative even if they aren't included in your final ROI estimate.
- **Time-effect**: Adoption of automation takes time; people overestimate it. You shouldn't rely just on perfect efficiency straight away. Plan a ramp-up period to fit the learning curve.

41 How Everything Harmonizes

Once your benefits have been quantified, organize them logically and persuasively. Sort them into three groups—strategic, indirect, and direct—then total them. Use visual aids such as pie graphs or bar charts to help one grasp the figures. Above importantly, relate the benefits to the aims of your company. Do you save money in finances? Raising client pleasure? About to start growing? Show how these numbers fairly represent the priorities of your stakeholders.

Automation is ultimately about more than only time or financial savings. All of it boils down to helping your business to be valuable. If you can precisely determine that value, your justification for moving forward will be more robust. Furthermore, the benefits will multiply depending on the right approach.

42   Assessing Risk and Uncertainty

Any job worth undertaking carries some degree of risk, though. Furthermore, automation initiatives are no exceptions. Technical problems, financial overruns, or team opposition are just a few of the several ways things may go south. The positive news is that, with time to predict them, dangers are controllable. Dealing with risk is about demonstrating to stakeholders that you have considered all the possible issues, are ready for difficulties, and have backup plans in place. It is not about solving every possible problem.

Developing a business case for automation presents a chance to demonstrate your credibility, rather than merely fulfilling a risk assessment requirement. Let's explore further the hazards you most certainly will come across and how to manage them.

43   Technical Risks: Will the Tech Perform as Anticipated?

Since technology forms the core of automation, it is not surprising that one of the main risk factors is a technical one. What would happen if the program failed to interface with your current systems? Should the program be buggy, erratic, or incapable of handling edge conditions? These are real problems that could lead to execution delays, increased expenses, or even the abandonment of the entire project—not just hypothetical ones. Consider, for instance, automating your AP (accounts payable) system. For simple invoices, the program runs flawlessly; nevertheless, it chokes on edge situations, such as invoices from foreign suppliers with different tax obligations. Your AP staff is now spending as much time addressing exceptions as they were completing the entire process manually. It's a typical example of technology not meeting expectations.

How, then, should one handle this? Begin with an exhaustive feasibility assessment. From the tools you now use to the processes you intend to automate, map out the technological terrain of your company. Pay particular attention to places like custom-built databases or older ERP systems where integration may be challenging.

Test once more before you commit. This is where a trial project can prevent costly surprises. Select a single, small-scale automated procedure to thoroughly test, then use the results to refine your strategy. Pilots allow you to identify issues early, before they escalate into more significant ones; these issues can include system incompatibilities, program limitations, or missing capabilities.

Finally, engage with reliable suppliers who have demonstrated success in your industry. Challenge their software's capabilities with challenging queries, then avoid accepting weak guarantees. Seek out case studies or references that showcase the application of their tools in environments similar to yours.

44   Operational risks: Will people use it correctly?

If humans do not embrace even the best automated tools, they are pointless. One of the most underappreciated hazards in every automated project is resistance to change. Workers may worry about bots replacing them or about losing their employment. Others may find learning a new system overwhelming or dubious of its advantages. If your team doesn't fully support the project, it will limit its impact, if not completely undermine it.

Imagine a consumer service division using a chatbot to answer simple questions. Should human agents doubt the correctness of the chatbot, they could find themselves personally rechecking responses and, therefore, repeating its efforts. Instead of saving time, the team wastes it, leading to the perception of the automation project as a failure.

To overcome this, begin involving staff members immediately. You shouldn't implement automation as a top-down directive. Instead, let your staff help you pinpoint problems and create answers. Employees who feel like they have a voice are more likely to view automation as a tool to assist them—not as a replacement.

One other important tactic is to present automation as a facilitator. Emphasize how automation will liberate them from monotonous, repetitive tasks, allowing them to focus on more significant tasks, thereby simplifying their responsibilities. For instance, demonstrate how automating data entry can free up time for creative problem-solving or customer contact.

Don't underestimate the importance of support and instruction. Some onboarding is even required of the most user-friendly technologies. Provide hands-on training courses, compile concise documentation, and ensure the rollout's support infrastructure for queries and issues is in place.

45   Financial Risks: Will it stay on budget and provide ROI?

Let's talk about money, which is typically the primary concern of most stakeholders. What happens if expenses spiral out of control? What happens if the benefits take longer than expected? Projects involving automation carry financial uncertainty, much as any investment does. Erroneous cost estimates or too-high benefits projections can sink even the most exciting projects.

Starting with thorough cost research helps one avoid such a situation. Beyond the obvious costs, there are software licenses and installation fees.

Consider hidden expenses (downtime, integration, and process redesign) and continuous expenses (maintenance, training, and scalability). Including a contingency buffer—say, 10 to 20 percent of your budget—allows you flexibility for unanticipated costs. Sensitivity analysis is another approach for control of financial risk. This involves verifying your ROI computations under various conditions. If adoption rates, for instance, fall short of projections, what happens? Alternatively, should the program deviate from expectations by 10% in cost? Modeling best-case, worst-case, and most-likely scenarios will enable you to show a spectrum of results that facilitate financial risk and reward understanding for stakeholders.

46   Strategic Risks: Will They Match Objectives Over Long Term?

Many businesses make the mistake of automating a procedure solely for its showiness or simplicity, without considering its overall impact. Automation for its own sake seldom adds long-lasting value. One simple inquiry will help you prevent this: Does this project fit our strategic goals?

Automating a customer service procedure, for instance, may lower response times, but if your company's main objective is to increase its product line, such automation might not be very helpful. Conversely, automating inventory control in readiness for increased manufacturing could have enormous strategic worth. Here, alignment is important. Make sure a process supports the long-term goals of your business before you decide to automate it. Seek chances that not only show quick return on investment but also set your company ready for future expansion, scalability, or competitiveness.

47   Dealing with Uncertainty: What You Don't Know (Yet)

Uncertainty is about the unknown, not about known obstacles; it differs from danger. Changing market conditions, shifting client tastes, or new technology may affect your automation project in ways you never would have imagined.
Plan with flexibility to negotiate uncertainties. Select instruments and techniques with outstanding adaptability, scalability, and simplicity of change. A chatbot platform that lets you adjust scripts on the fly, for instance, will be more robust to shifting consumer questions than a rigid, hard-coded solution.

Reevaluating often is another tactic. See your automation project as a continuous initiative rather than a one-time fix. See it regularly—say every three or six months—to assess its performance, streamline processes, and change with the times.

48   Presenting Risk and Uncertainty to Stakeholders

Stakeholders want preparation, not perfection. Present hazards honestly and clearly. Emphasize the hazards you have found, describe how you intend to reduce them, and—above all—showcase their possible influence.

"Integration might be an issue," for instance, might not be as effective as expressing, "There's a 20% chance that integrating the automation tool with our ERP system could take an additional two weeks, costing $5,000. To get at this, we have included a $10,000 cushion into the budget." This method not only shows your meticulous nature but also gives stakeholders hope that you have done research.

49   The Bottom Line

Though they seldom come without risk, automation projects are not dangerous either. The variation resides in your attitude toward them. Understanding the technological, operational, financial, and strategic risks—and having a strategy to control them—you can create a business case that is not only compelling but also flawless. Ultimately, it's about proving you're ready to face obstacles rather than about totally avoiding them. That is how ideas become action and mistrust becomes confidence.

50 ROI Calculation and Presentation

Calculating ROI for process automation involves crafting a narrative using these statistics, rather than relying solely on numerical calculations. It should address concerns, convince decision-makers, and pave the path for action. Beyond a formula, you must delve into the specifics: where the expenses originate, how the benefits stack up, and what hazards or uncertainty might affect the outcome. This part is all about combining such elements and presenting them in an intriguing rather than only logical manner.

51 Framework for Calculation of ROI

The ROI estimate in your business case for automation is your compass, not only a figure. That number will persuade your stakeholders to say, "Yes, let's do this." Still, ROI is more than a calculation. It's a technique of realizing the interaction among time, expenses, and benefits and then presenting the outcomes in an understandable and convincing manner. ROI is about showing that the automation project is a good investment for your company, not just how much you'll save. This entails then dissecting it methodically, considering all the factors, and putting out a reasonable, defendable case. Let's delve deeper into the process of calculating the return on investment for process automation.

The starting point for ROI is straightforward:

$$ROI(\%) = \left(\frac{Net\ Benefits}{Total\ Costs}\right) * 100$$

Here's what the components mean:
- Net Benefits = Total Benefits less Total Costs

- Total Costs = Initial Costs + Recurring Costs + Hidden Costs
- First look at it appears straightforward enough. Enter your figures and obtain a percentage. Still, the real effort is in knowing what those figures represent. Every line item—those which costs money as well as benefits—must be dissected, examined, and supported by facts.

52   First Step: determining expenses

Let´s start on the simpler side of the equation—costs. Though they usually are more concrete than benefits, they still need careful thought. There are three main divisions to total costs:

- Initial costs including buying tools, configuring tools, and building infrastructure comprise upfront fees. Using an RPA system, for instance, may cost $30,000 for setup and consultation fees plus $50,000 for licensing.
- Automation is not a one-and-done investment. Maintenance, software upgrades, training, and scaling are among the recurring costs. These can call for a $5,000 annual training contract for new hires or a $10,000 annual maintenance contract.
- Hidden expenses are those that, although not necessarily obvious in your first estimates, can have a major influence. What happens, for example, should you have downtime during implementation? Alternatively, if including legacy systems with automation technologies calls for more development effort?

The secret is to view holistically here. Explore the possible difficulties and consider them rather than concentrating only on the evident expenses. For instance, if your IT staff projects that adding a new automation tool will require three weeks of development work, consider your pay as part of the implementation cost.

53   Second Step: calculating advantages

The magic occurs when one quantifies benefits. This is the difference between automation as an expense and as an investment. But particularly when they involve indirect or intangible profits, benefits can be more difficult to evaluate than expenses.

Direct Benefits:
Since they relate to quantifiable results like time savings or error avoidance, direct benefits are the easiest to figure out. For instance:
- Use employee costs of $60,000 a year. Automating a process can save 1,000 hours, which equates to a savings of $30,000.
- If we reduce error rates by 90%, we can save an additional $45,000 by lowering rework expenses from $50,000 to $5,000 annually.

Indirect Benefits:
Though less clear-cut, these are nonetheless rather vital. They include things like faster client response times, which increases retention rates, or better staff satisfaction—which lowers turnover expenses. As one illustration:
Automating tedious processes could reduce staff turnover by 10%, saving $20,000 in training and recruitment costs.

Strategic advantages:
Though they won't always show up right away, these advantages will help your company over time. Think about scalability, agility, and enhanced compliance. As follows:
Though the financial return takes time to show, if automation lets your team manage a 50% increase in volume without increasing workers, that's a big benefit.
Quantifying advantages calls for supporting your figures with facts. Support your presumptions with industry norms, past performance, or standards. And be conservative when in doubt. If real outcomes fall short, overpromising benefits might harm your reputation.

54 Third Step: Factor in Time

Projects involving automation can ask for large initial or upfront costs, so advantages are usually built over time. For this reason, ROI is not only about the net benefit, but also about the time at which you see this benefit. The payback period is one helpful indicator here:

$$Payback\ Period = \frac{Initial\ Investment}{Annual\ Net\ Benefits}$$

The payback time, for instance, is two years if an automation project costs $100,000 initially and produces $50,000 in yearly net benefits. This tells interested parties how long it will take to get back to the start. To consider the temporal worth of money, you can also apply instruments like Internal Rate of Return (IRR) or Net Present worth (NPV). For initiatives with long-term gains especially, these indicators are quite helpful.

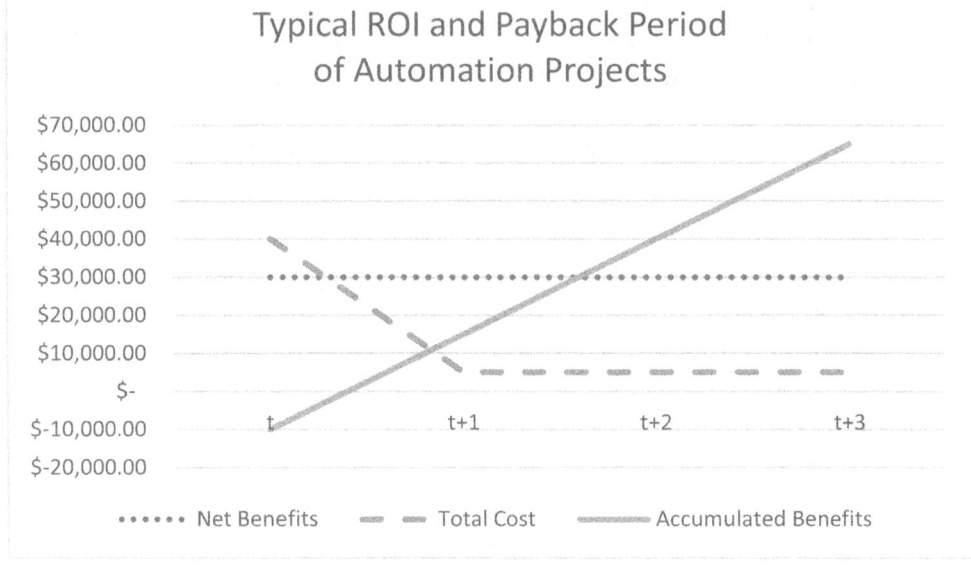

Figure 4: ROI and Payback Period of Automation Projects

Figure 4: ROI and Payback Period of Automation ProjectsFigure 4 shows an example of ROI and Payback Period. Looking first at the total costs, these are high at the beginning (t), but then decrease significantly. This is due to the initial costs, which are only incurred at the beginning. In t+1 and following periods, they are replaced by the recurring costs, which are significantly lower. The net benefits remain the same, here $30,000. This results in the accumulated benefits. These increase over time and become positive over time.

55 Fourth Step: Conduct a sensitivity analysis

"What if your assumptions are wrong?" is one of the most often used refutes to ROI calculations. Here is where a sensitivity analysis finds application. Modeling several scenarios helps you demonstrate how ROI varies depending on the situation.

- Best Case: With a ROI of 180%, benefits exceed predicted by 10%.
- Worst Case: Adoption is delayed and expenses are 20% greater, so producing a ROI of 50%.
- Most likely case: one in which the ROI is balanced at 120%.
- And so on

This method not only shows thoroughness but also helps one to have confidence that one has considered uncertainty.

56   Fifth Step: Present the Numbers Clearly

Presenting ROI in a way your audience will find relevant comes last once you have computed it. Most stakeholders, remember, want the big picture rather than seeing every single item. Give particular attention to:

- The Headlines Metric: Work from the payback time or general ROI percentage first. "This project will deliver 150% ROI over three years with a payback period of 18 months."
- Key Drivers: Emphasize the primary efficiency increases or cost savings behind the return on investment. "We'll save $200,000 annually in labor and rework costs by automating invoice processing."
- Visual Aid: Use tables, graphs, or charts to break out difficult information. A bar chart contrasting costs and benefits over time, for instance, can demonstrate the speed with which the investment pays off.

57   An Illustration in Action

Assume for the moment you are automating the "new employee onboarding process". The figures might show this:

- Software will cost upfront $30,000 and implementation will cost $30,000.
- Maintenance expenses run $5,000 a year from year 2 on.
- Thus, three years' total costs come to $70,000.
- Automation saves 1,000 hours yearly at $25/hour, or $25,000/year.
- Less mistakes mean $10,000 year in rework savings.
- Increased retention brought on by employee satisfaction saves $5,000 annually.
- Thus, three years: $120,000 total benefits.

ROI:

$$ROI(\%) = \left(\frac{Net\ Benefits(120{,}000 - 70{,}000)}{Total\ Costs(70{,}000)}\right) * 100 = 71\%$$

The payback period would be just under 2 years.

58 The Final Thought

Finding ROI is about conveying a story with numbers, not only a mathematical issue. You may create a business case that is not only strong but also impregnable by separating expenses, measuring benefits, and including time and uncertainty. Your stakeholders will be more confident in you as the more methodically and open you are. And that's how you move ROI from a calculation into a green light for action.

59 Making a Strong Business Case

To be clear, a business case is not only a gathering of facts, figures, and buzzwords. This story shows stakeholders why your automated project is desirable and necessary. The objective is to convince, inspire, and motivate action, not only to offer knowledge. Done correctly, your business case will make clear to your audience that this project is the wise one for the company. But creating a solid business case calls for more than just putting an ROI computation on a PowerPoint slide. You need to connect the figures to real-world problems, anticipate queries before they arise, and craft a compelling presentation for your audience. Let us dissect it methodically here.

60 Start with the Why: Clearly define the Problem

Every excellent business case begins with a problem, quite obviously. Your audience won't act if they don't see the problem or consider it urgent. Your first responsibility is to succinctly and clearly state the issue together with supporting evidence from data. Suppose, for instance, you are presenting automation for your customer service division. Rather than declaring, "Our processes are inefficient," create a clear picture:

"Our customer care team now spends forty percent of its time responding to common queries like "Where's my order?" and "How do I return this item?" Longer waiting times and worse customer satisfaction follow because less time is available for addressing difficult problems. Over the past year, our net promoter score (NPS) has declined from 70 to 62."

By defining the problem in quantifiable terms such as time lost, client discontent, and wasted effort, you instantly establish the urgency. Before they are ready to learn about the fix, stakeholders must experience suffering.

61   The Solution: Position Automation as Fix

Present your solution after you have clearly defined the issue. Here, the main emphasis should be on results rather than just the technology itself. Your audience cares more about what a chatbot or RPA bot can do than how it works:

"We can automatically address seventy percent of repeated questions by using an AI-powered chatbot. This will enable our human agents to concentrate on challenging customer problems, therefore lowering average response times ranging from 24 hours to 6 hours and raising customer satisfaction."

This approach emphasizes results—faster response times, happier consumers, and more efficient staff—right now. Keep it straightforward and outcome-oriented; relate the answer straight to the just-mentioned problem.

62   Count the advantages and make the value very clear

Your business case revolves around this. Stakeholders seek clarity regarding the value they are receiving for their investment, and numerical data assists in highlighting the advantages. The more precise you can be, the better. Start with the most definite, quantifiable advantages:

- Savings in Cost: Determine by cutting labor expenses, removing mistakes, or accelerating procedures how much automation will save. For instance, "We'll save 1,200 hours yearly, equivalent to $36,000 in labor costs, by automating our payroll process."
- Efficiency Boosts: Calculate the time saved, then, if at all possible, translate it into cash. "Automating invoice

processing will cut the average processing time from 10 minutes to 2 minutes, freeing 800 hours annually."
- Income Effects: If automation can promote income growth—through faster sales cycles, better client retention, or enhanced upselling—,spell it out. "Reducing customer service response times by 50% could increase retention rates by 5%, adding $150,000 in annual revenue."

Don't stop at advantages straightforwardly. Include strategic and indirect value as well.

- Faster, more precise procedures create happier consumers; hence, they strengthen retention and loyalty.
- Automating tiresome chores helps workers concentrate on more important work, reducing burnout and turnover.
- Automation lets you manage expansion without a commensurate rise in head count.

This section should leave readers wondering, "How could we not do this?"

63   Talk about the risks; be honest

Like any undertaking, automation carries some risk. Acting otherwise will actually lead to a decrease in stakeholder confidence, not an increase. A solid business case demonstrates that you have considered risks and have a strategy to control them rather than merely noting them.

Risk: "Employees could reject using the new system."
Mitigation: "We'll address this by involving employees in the design process, offering hands-on training, and stressing how automation will cut their workload."

Risk: "Integration with our legacy CRM system could take longer than expected."

Mitigation: "We have allocated a contingency budget of $15,000 for additional development resources if required."

You show not only foresight but also management by organizing hazards and their remedies. Seeing that you have anticipated potential challenges will help stakeholders trust your strategy.

64   Share a Story: Link the Dots

Though they are fundamental, numbers are insufficient on their own. A solid business case combines those facts into a narrative showing how automation will move the company from its present difficulties to a better future.

For example:
- "Our finance team spends 20 hours a week manually reconciling invoices, delaying month-end reporting and raising error rates."
- "Automation will handle 90% of the reconciliation process, therefore saving two hours every week from the time needed."
- "This will free up 936 hours annually, equivalent to $28,000 in labor costs, and ensure error-free reporting."

Your business case becomes more accessible and memorable if you arrange it as a story. Visualizing the change helps stakeholders to support it more probably.

65 Customize the Message by Understanding Your Audience

Various stakeholders have varied priorities; hence your business case should represent those of different interests. While the COO would be more concerned with operational efficiency, the CFO may concentrate on financial measures including payback times and ROI. Making your message fit your readers guarantees it will be interesting.

For example: "This project will deliver a 120% ROI over three years, with a payback period of just 18 months," for the CFO.

"Automating our warehouse operations will reduce order processing times by 50%, allowing us to handle a 30% increase in volume without adding staff," for the COO.

You help each stakeholder to see the value from their point of view by attending to their priorities.

66 Finish with a call-to-action directive

A good business case doesn't leave your audience puzzled about their next move. It closes with unambiguous, doable advice. For example: "Investing $100,000 in this automation project will yield net advantages of $200,000 over three years. With a goal go-live date of April 1, we suggest beginning with a pilot phase concentrated on the payroll process."

This kind of ending connects everything and offers a road map for next developments. It guarantees that everyone is in line on the forthcoming actions and reflects confidence.

67   The Bottom Line

A business case is a tool for decision-making not only a paperwork item. Defining the problem, estimating the advantages, managing risks, and offering a clear road forward can help you not only argue for automation but also make it difficult to say no. Your business case will determine how likely you are to realize your automation project from a concept. And there is where the actual value starts.

68 Presenting ROI to Stakeholders

Making the pitch comes at last. This is about generating confidence rather than only proving your arithmetic. The individuals in the room must believe that you are the one to bring about this project since it is the right one.

Best practices for presenting ROI:

- **Lead with the headline first:**
  Starting with your most interesting figure, "this project will deliver 177% ROI over three years with a payback period of just over one year."
- **Go through the process like walking:**
  Describe, in brief, how you computed benefits and expenses. Show your work; but, unless asked, avoid becoming mired in the specifics.
- **Predict Questions:**
  Be ready to answer questions including "What if costs overrun?" or "How do we know employees will adopt this?" Get ready with responses beforehand.
- **Execute scenarios:**
  Show under several presumptions how the ROI holds up. "Even if benefits are 20% lower than expected, we still achieve a positive ROI within two years."

Managing Conflicts:
- Should they say, "It's too risky," stress your pilot project and strategies for risk reduction.
- If they ask "Can we afford it?" stress the long-term savings and payback times.
- Should they object to adoption, explain how you will guide and equip staff members.

The Takeaway
ROI is the basis of your argument; it is more than just numbers. Together with a bold, clear presentation, a well-considered ROI may transform ideas into action and doubters into supporters. Although automation involves high upfront costs, it pays off in the right situation, and much more besides.

69 Practical Case Studies and Insights

70 Case Studies of Successful Automation Projects

Case studies are the unsung heroes of any automation business case. Although risk analyses and return on investment estimates are vital, nothing compares to the ability of a real-world case to bring your idea to life. Case studies highlight the difficulties, show what automation looks like in action—they prove it works. Above all, they show what previous companies have accomplished and how, therefore offering a road map for success.

Presenting case studies calls for more than just enumeration of outcomes. You must show stakeholders that, should it work for someone else, it will work for you by tying their experiences to your objectives. Let's examine thorough cases of successful automation and learn how to properly apply case studies.

71 Why Should Case Studies Count?

Case studies help your idea to be credible by being firmly anchored in reality. They explain how actual companies have carried out similar initiatives and produced quantifiable outcomes, therefore transforming automation from an abstract idea into a practical answer. This realization that your proposal has undergone testing and verification, rather than being merely theoretical, can serve as a pivotal moment for skeptics. Particularly helpful are case studies since they:

- Show results that include specific instances of cost savings, efficiency increases, and other advantages, supported by actual figures

- Draw attention to difficult tasks. They not only highlight successes but also indicate challenges that were surmounted, fostering faith in the viability of your own initiative
- Provide a road map, showing what worked (and what didn't), thereby guiding your own strategy

72 Presenting Case Studies: Effective Approach

Structure case studies in a clear, relevant, outcome-oriented manner to maximize their value. Here is the process:

- **Start with the problem**: Describe the company's prior pain issues before automation. This prepares your audience to relate with the difficulties.
- **Specify the solution in detail**: Describe how the company addressed the issue via automation. Emphasize their actions rather than only their equipment.
- **Emphasize the Achievements**: Show the observable results of automation, wherever it is feasible utilizing data. Add qualitative advantages (such as happier employees, better customer experience) as well as quantitative ones (like time or money saved).
- **Relate the case study back to your own circumstances**: Emphasize commonalities in procedures, objectives, or obstacles to help to explain why this example is pertinent.
-

73   Case Study 1: processing invoices automatically in a SMC

Problem:
A mid-sized manufacturing company was overwhelmed by its accounts payable (AP) process. With each invoice averaging 15 minutes to evaluate, match with a purchase order, and enter into the ERP system, the AP team manually handled more than 3,000 invoices a month. About 10% of invoices needed rework, and mistakes were prevalent; delays caused late payment penalties and threatened vendor relationships.

Solution:
The company automated the whole billing process using an RPA platform. The bot inserted authorized invoices straight into the ERP system, matched data from invoices with purchase orders, noted disparities for hand inspection.

Results:
- Processing invoices was reduced from 15 to 3 minutes, saving around 600 hours a month.
- Labor expenses dropped by $180,000 a year.
- Rework expenditure decreased by $50,000 annually when error rates dropped by 90%.
- On-time payment rates raised by 40% helped to build confidence and negotiating power with important vendors.

Takeaways:
This case study is the ideal illustration of how automation changes a high-volume, repetitious task such as invoice processing. Should your company suffer with comparable inefficiencies, the possible return on investment is obvious.

74   Case Study 2: AI Chatbots in Consumer Service for Retailers

Problem:
A rapidly expanding online retailer was finding it difficult to answer consumer questions. Handling an average of 5,000 questions every week, the customer support crew was overburdened and 60% of inquiries concentrated on repeated problems such account changes, purchase tracking, and return policies. Long response times—averaging 24 hours—caused an increase in customer complaints and a decline in Net Promoter Score (NPS) from 75 to 60.

Solution:
The company used a chatbot driven by artificial intelligence to answer routine questions. To collect real-time order data and give consumers instantaneous answers, the chatbot was connected to their CRM system.

Results:
- For regular searches, average response times reduced from 24 hours to less than one minute.
- The chatbot answered 70% of tickets on its own, therefore saving $250,000 yearly in personnel costs and lessening of support team effort.
- NPS recovered from 60 to 78 during six months.
- Scalability: The chatbot easily managed a 50% increase in ticket volume without additional staff during busiest holiday seasons.

Takeaways:
If your customer support staff is overburdened with repeated questions, chatbots can provide fast wins by lowering response times and thereby saving expenses. They also offer a scalable answer for seasonal or unplanned demand increases.

75   Case Study 3: Financial Services Automating Compliance Reporting

The challenge was increasing regulatory pressure on a regional bank whose quarterly compliance reporting needed hundreds of hours of manual data collecting, validation, and formatting. The system was prone to mistakes; missing deadlines would cause fines and loss of reputation. Stretched thin, the compliance staff spent 80% of their time on repeated reporting chores rather than strategic projects.

Solution:
To expedite the compliance procedure, the bank installed a workflow automation solution. The system created reports in the necessary forms, automatically gathered data from several systems, and applied validation standards.

Results:
- Reporting time fell from 400 hours every quarter to 50 hours, allowing 350 hours for strategic work.
- Automation guaranteed perfect regulatory compliance, therefore removing fines and penalties.
- The compliance team noted better job satisfaction since they could concentrate on value-added activities rather than hand-made manual work.

Takeaways:
Automation provides time savings and peace of mind even if regulatory compliance is a hassle. This case study shows how workflow automation might cut risk, remove repetitious chores, and raise staff morale.

76 Combining All the Components

Case studies are a tool to engage your audience rather than only a means of highlighting what is possible. Presenting actual cases of successful automation helps the idea to be concrete and relevant. More importantly, you demonstrate to stakeholders that there are known answers for their problems; they are not unique.

Always relate case studies back to the objectives of your own company. Emphasize similarities, demonstrate how outcomes can be attained, and place your automation project as the next natural development. By doing this, you increase confidence rather than merely creating a business case. And that is what brings concepts to life.

77   Industry-Specific ROI Insights

Every industry has unique dynamics, problems, and possibilities; therefore, automation solutions must mirror that reality. Although efficiency, cost savings, and scalability—the main benefits of automation—applicate everywhere, the details of where and how they provide value vary greatly. Maximizing ROI and guaranteeing success depend on customizing automation to meet needs particular to a sector.

Let's investigate how automation plays out in important sectors, revealing special opportunities and obstacles, and proving how companies have used it to get significant outcomes.

78   From Reactive to Predictive Manufacturing

Manufacturing has been at the forefront of automation, particularly for non-software automation, but its potential extends far beyond the factory floor. While digital automation tools are currently revolutionizing inventory control, supply chain coordination, and equipment maintenance, physical robots have revolutionized assembly lines.

Many factories find controlling downtime to be difficult. The unexpected breakdown of machines can cost hundreds, if not millions, of dollars, stopping manufacturing and upsetting supply lines. Often ineffective are conventional maintenance techniques, either planned or reactive repairs. Machine learning algorithms and Internet of Things (IoT) sensors drive predictive maintenance. These tools track machinery in real time, spotting possible breakdowns before they start and planning preventative repairs.

For example, a global auto parts company implemented predictive maintenance using IoT in all its plants. Consequently, unplanned downtime dropped by thirty percent, saving $500,000 a year. Automating inventory control also guaranteed that raw supplies were exactly accessible when needed, therefore minimizing surplus inventory and saving still another $200,000 yearly. These successes resulted from not only improved efficiency but also from building an agile, more robust operation.

79   Healthcare: Reducing the Administrative Workload

In healthcare, where every dollar and every second count, automation provides a lifeline. The industry's dual challenges of strict regulatory compliance and substantial administrative expenses create ideal opportunities for process simplification. Although clinical uses of artificial intelligence, such as tailored treatment and diagnosis, are making news, automating routine but necessary administrative chores usually yields an instant return on investment.

Examine billing and patient intake. For insurance claims, appointment scheduling, and medical records, hospitals and clinics frequently rely on manual data entry, which causes inefficiencies and lets expensive mistakes through. By automating these processes, accuracy increases in addition to operations speed-up.

For instance, a major hospital network implemented automated billing, which resulted in a halving of processing times. By speeding reimbursements, this adjustment increased cash flow, cut errors by 90%, and avoided $300,000 in yearly rework expenses. To free up its front desk employees to concentrate on more valuable contacts with patients, the hospital recently unveiled a chatbot for appointment scheduling. This little change had a significant effect: patient satisfaction ratings rose by 15%, and the hospital saved $100,000 a year on labor expenses.

These administrative successes set the stage for future attempts at clinical automation scale-building. Often the fastest approach to return on investment in healthcare begins with back-office automation.

80   Financial Services: Compliance and Beyond

Few sectors face regulatory scrutiny as strongly as financial services. The stakes couldn't be greater given mounds of data to handle, rigorous deadlines to satisfy, and ongoing risk of audits or fines. Automation presents a means of more precisely and effectively managing compliance reporting, fraud detection, and customer onboarding.

One excellent model comes from a regional bank. The compliance staff of the bank was previously responsible for manually aggregating data for anti-money laundering (AML) reports, a task that required 400 hours per quarter. Workflow automation reduced the reporting procedure to just 50 hours. This minimized the possibility of mistakes that would cause regulatory fines and freed 350 hours per quarter for the team to concentrate on other important chores. Faster audit trails made possible by automation also help reduce risk by increasing bank operational confidence. Automation in financial services is generating value in fraud detection that extends beyond compliance. Using machine learning techniques, a credit card issuer examined transaction trends and raised real-time potential fraud warnings. Fraud losses reduced 25% in a year, saving about $1 million.
Here, the lesson is: automation enables strategic innovation, lowers risk, and improves trust in addition to helping to minimize expenses.

81   Retail: Improving Consumer Experience

Customers experience rules in the retail sector; thus, automation is transforming this sector as well. Every touchpoint—from order fulfillment and customer service to inventory control—offers chances for development.

Examine the inventory control challenge. While excess ties up capital and storage space, stockouts cause lost sales. A large retailer utilized AI-backed demand forecasting to optimize its inventory. The algorithm accurately forecasted stock needs by examining seasonality, geographical preferences, and sales trends. The company therefore cut inventory holding expenses by 20%, saving $300,000 yearly and guaranteeing always available popular products.

RPA systems accelerated order fulfillment in the warehouse, therefore lowering processing times by 40%. Regarding customer support, a chatbot answered basic questions such as order tracking and return policy, therefore lightening agent workload and accelerating response times. These combined improvements raised customer satisfaction levels and helped the store save $500,000 in annual labor costs.

Automation's benefits in retail usually show up as happier consumers. More loyalty and more sales follow from faster service, correct stock levels, and tailored recommendations.

82   Small and Medium Businesses (SMBs): Stretching Resources

Automation is not only a good-to-have but also a survival tactic for SMBs. Tight budgets and limited resources force efficiency to be a major concern; automation lets fewer teams accomplish more with less.

Think of a consulting SMB. The company faced problems due to manual invoicing, which resulted in stretched cash flow and delayed payments. The business reduced payment delays by 30% and increased cash flow by $50,000/year by automating the invoicing process.

Another tiny e-commerce company sent customized email campaigns using marketing automation, therefore boosting open rates by 25% and generating $100,000 in extra sales. Off-the-shelf automation technologies like QuickBooks for accountancy or Zapier for app integration usually help SMBs the most. For companies looking for rapid gains, these reasonably priced, simple-to-apply, scalable solutions are perfect.

83   The Big Picture: Emphasize What Matters Most

Every sector has different difficulties, but the ideas of automation success are the same: concentrate on activities that have the most impact, match automation to your strategic objectives, and track performance in terms of observable outcomes. Automation can revolutionize how companies run, from lowering production downtime to lowering compliance costs in financial services to satisfy consumers in retail.

When sharing these ideas with stakeholders, link your own company's requirements to industry case studies. Show how similar approaches could produce similar outcomes, and frame automation not only as a basis for long-term success but also as a solution to present issues.

84 Bringing It All Together

Calculating the ROI of process automation initiatives is a means of thinking about how technology may radically change your company, not only a mathematical exercise. We have looked at the mechanics of ROI, the techniques for spotting prospects, and the ways to create a strong business case in this book. It's time now to stand back and consider the wider picture: what does it mean to project ROI for automation, and how may this paradigm help you achieve long-term, sustainable success?

85 ROI as the Strategic Lens

ROI goes beyond a figure. You figure out how to get a project authorized. It provides a prism through which you may assess how automation really affects your company. This method compels you to consider risks, rewards, and expenses critically. Whether your company's larger objectives are cost control, expansion, or enhanced customer experience, it motivates you to match automation projects with those aims.

Still, ROI also has to do with priorities. Not every tool will add value; not every task is worth automating. You make sure your automation initiatives are focused and powerful by concentrating on the procedures and processes with the best possible returns—those that are repetitious, rule-based, and high-volume. This orderly method helps to avoid waste of resources and generates enthusiasm for the next initiatives.

86 From Statistics to Action

Understanding the ROI marks only the first stage. The actual difficulty is putting those real insights into use. E.g., the most effective automation projects become part of a larger transformation plan rather than ending at one project. It's important to consider scaling once you have demonstrated the advantages of automation through a high-impact project or pilot effort.

Seek patterns first. Should one part of your accounts payable process show notable returns on investment, what additional financial processes can profit from such tools? Should a chatbot provide better customer service, how might artificial intelligence improve other aspects of consumer experience? When automation is combined throughout the company, it creates synergies that magnify the benefits.

87 Anticipating Change

Automation is dynamic. Tools change, corporate needs change, and the state of the market moves. Remember that the presumptions you started a project with could not stay valid as you keep investigating fresh prospects. This is where ongoing measurement finds application. Tracking important performance indicators and matching real data to your ROI forecasts can help you to improve your strategy and guarantee that every new project builds on the success of the last.

For instance, suppose your first automated project concentrated on lowering payroll mistakes. You projected a 50% decrease, but the real improvement is more like 30%. After implementation, too. Why did the discrepancy arise? Was training lacking in some areas? A restriction in a program? Knowing these subtleties not only helps you maximize the present project but also offers great knowledge for next projects.

88   The Broad Effects of Automation

Calculations of return on investment can center on instantaneous, observable gains like time savings or financial savings. True benefit of automation, however, goes much beyond the balance sheet. It's about changing the way your company runs: enabling staff members to concentrate on important tasks, improve customer experience, and build a basis for expansion. Take a manufacturing facility that used predictive maintenance to lower downtime. Though the cultural influence was equally great, the financial savings were notable. Workers were able to concentrate on creativity and process enhancement instead of rushing to repair unanticipated equipment breakdowns. In healthcare, too, automating administrative chores not only saves money but also lets providers spend more time with patients, therefore enhancing results and happiness.

Although they are more difficult to measure, these knock-on effects are equally vital than the hard figures. Do not hesitate to add qualitative advantages to your business case together with numerical measures. Stakeholders must get the whole picture of what automation is capable of.

89   A Call to Action

If there is one major takeaway from this book, it is that automation is a strategy rather than only a tool. Approaching ROI with discipline and rigor can help you to go past the hoopla and concentrate on initiatives that really show value. Still, success cannot be found in numbers by themselves. It results from challenging your staff, posing appropriate questions, and matching automation to the requirements of your company.

Remember as you proceed:

- Though you start small, think large. One effective initiative can set the foundation for a transformation across a business.
- Check everything. Your best friend in proving ROI, spotting opportunities, and enhancing performance is data.
- Get flexible. The corporate environment is continually changing; hence your automation plan should also change.

Above all, be not reluctant to leap forward. Those companies who embrace automation deliberately will be the ones who flourish in a world that is going more and more digital. Your road map is ROI; but the route starts with activity.

90 The Road Ahead

One thing strikes me quite clearly as I consider the trip we have traveled across this book: automation—more especially, the emergence of AI—has transformative power. Automation serves not just as a tool, but also as a force that can revolutionize the operations of companies, human behavior, and the potential for innovation. The opportunities are unlimited. AI can anticipate what we would never dream of, analyze trends humans cannot perceive, and adapt to difficulties we would find difficult to articulate. The enormous majority of businesses, however, are not ready to fully seize these possibilities.

This is not due to a lack of ambition or interest. AI is undeniably appealing, prompting leaders worldwide to embrace it. However, it should be noted that artificial intelligence is not a panacea for outpacing competitors or addressing inefficiencies. This is a sophisticated instrument that excels on orderly, well-specified procedures. Even the most advanced AI programs will falter without a solid basis.

This is where process automation, which has been extensively discussed in this book, becomes useful. Businesses must solve the fundamental anarchy in their systems before they can fully exploit AI. Though not fancy, it's essential. Every day in companies, hundreds, perhaps thousands, of repetitious, manual operations are performed, depleting resources, impeding innovation, and hiding the very possibilities that artificial intelligence is supposed to find.

Imagine trying to train AI to maximize your supply chain while inventory tracking still depends on prone-to-error spreadsheets. Consider the scenario where you attempt to implement predictive analytics in customer service, only to find your staff members bogged down in addressing basic, repetitive queries. AI requires structure. To provide its claimed value, it requires consistent input, well-defined policies, and effective procedures.

This is precisely why rule-based automation should serve as the foundation for AI.

Businesses accomplish two important goals by initially automating tedious chores first—those simple, rule-based operations that clutter every department. They first free their human staff to concentrate on the creative, strategic, and relationship-driven jobs AI enhances but does not replace. Second, they establish orderly, predictable procedures that might provide raw materials for AI-driven invention. When you automate, efficiently, and error-free your processes, you are not expecting AI to tackle simple problems. Rather, you are enabling it to maximize and invent at a level not possible for humans alone.

Let's not rush to center AI in every choice, every process, and every encounter. Rather, let us approach this deliberately and with discipline; begin with the foundations. Automate what is manual; eliminate what is superfluous; and improve what is ineffective. Create a culture of ongoing development so automation is not only a one-time initiative but a way of thinking. This work guarantees AI flourishes when it eventually takes the stage. Too many companies have succumbed to the hype and use AI without laying the necessary foundation, resulting in costly instruments that have no practical use. It's a lack of preparation, not a technological shortcoming. The positive news is that every company, regardless of size or sector, can lay this basis. It begins with a dedication to structure, method, and the long game. This is about grasping their interaction, not about choosing between AI and automation. While AI lifts those processes by learning, adjusting, and optimizing, automation sets the foundation by standardizing and streamlining tasks. Combined, they produce a continuum of change capable of redefining corporate possibilities.

Closing this book, I want you to consider: for those who are ready, the future is bright. While the majority of the work is being done in the background, AI has the potential to be the primary focus. Whether AI is a game-changer or merely another trend will depend on the hundreds of little changes, the removal of inefficiencies, and the constant attention on improved procedures.

Thus, let us welcome the chances that lie ahead, but let us do it deliberately and with aim. Start with automation. Always keep optimizing. And when you're ready, let AI carry you beyond what you could have ever imagined. That is the direction forward. There is a path worth taking here.

91 App.: Key Learnings of the Book in a Nutshell

1. **Understand the Foundations of ROI:**
   - ROI is a vital metric for evaluating the feasibility and profitability of automation projects. Understanding its components—costs, benefits, and timeframes—is essential for accuracy.

2. **Identify the Right Processes:**
   - Not every process is suited for automation. Focus on repetitive, high-volume, rule-based tasks with clear inefficiencies to maximize ROI.

3. **Build a Robust Business Case:**
   - Comprehensive cost and benefit analysis, risk assessment, and a structured ROI calculation are the backbone of a persuasive business case.

4. **Leverage Practical Examples:**
   - Real-world case studies demonstrate that automation can deliver significant financial and operational benefits across industries when implemented thoughtfully.

5. **Adapt to Industry-Specific Needs:**
   - Tailor your approach to align with the unique challenges and opportunities in your industry, whether it's manufacturing, healthcare, finance, or retail.

92 App.: Resources for Estimating and Maximizing ROI

To ensure your automation projects succeed, it's critical to have the right tools, frameworks, and resources at your disposal. The following resources have been curated to help you at every stage of the process, from identifying opportunities and calculating ROI to implementing solutions and tracking their impact.

Frameworks and Methodologies: Detailed Exploration
Frameworks and methodologies form the backbone of any successful automation initiative, especially when it comes to estimating ROI and planning execution. These tools provide structured approaches to evaluate processes, identify opportunities, and calculate value with precision. Here, we'll take a deeper dive into each suggested framework and methodology, explaining their purpose, how they work, and why they're critical for automation success.

93 ROI Calculation Frameworks

Payback Period Calculator
- **What It Is:** A straightforward formula that calculates how long it will take for the benefits of your automation project to recover the costs.

- **How It Works:**

$$Payback\ Period = \frac{Total\ Investment\ Cost}{Annual\ Net\ Benefits}$$

This means, if your automation project costs $100,000 upfront and generates $50,000 in annual net benefits, your payback period is 2 years.

The components of total investment costs were explained in Part 2 and include in particular one-off and ongoing costs. The annual net benefits also result from the sum of the (quantified) benefits explained in Part 2.
- **Why It Matters:** This simple metric provides a clear timeline for when the project will break even, which is especially useful for stakeholders focused on short-term financial goals.

Net Present Value (NPV) and Internal Rate of Return (IRR) Models

- **What They Are:**

    o NPV measures the difference between the present value of cash inflows (benefits) and cash outflows (costs) over the project's lifecycle.

    o IRR calculates the discount rate at which the project's NPV equals zero, effectively showing its expected return.

- **How They Work:**

    o $NPV = \sum_{t=1}^{n} \frac{Net\ Cash\ Flow}{(1+r)^t} - Initial\ Investment$
    where r is the discount rate and t is the time period.

    o IRR is derived by iterating discount rates until NPV = 0.

- **Why They Matter:** These models help you evaluate long-term projects, taking into account the time value of money, making them ideal for automation initiatives with ongoing benefits.

Sensitivity Analysis Templates
- **What It Is:** A framework to test how changes in assumptions (e.g., cost, benefit, adoption rate) affect ROI.

- **How It Works:** Create scenarios like best-case, worst-case, and most-likely outcomes by adjusting variables and recalculating ROI.
    - For example, what happens if labor savings are 20% lower than expected? Or if upfront costs increase by 10%?
- **Why It Matters:** By visualizing the range of potential outcomes, sensitivity analysis helps you prepare for uncertainty and build stakeholder confidence.

94 Automation Suitability Frameworks

Automation Potential Matrix
- **What It Is:** A two-axis matrix that evaluates processes based on complexity (low to high) and volume (low to high).
- **How It Works:**
    - **Low Complexity, High Volume:** These processes (e.g., invoice processing) are the easiest and most valuable to automate.
    - **High Complexity, Low Volume:** These may require specialized tools or be better suited for partial automation.
- **Why It Matters:** This framework helps prioritize automation efforts by focusing on processes that deliver the highest ROI with minimal risk.

Process Mapping Methodologies
- **What They Are:** Techniques like Lean Six Sigma or BPMN (Business Process Model and Notation) for visualizing workflows and identifying inefficiencies.

- **How They Work:**
    - Use flowcharts or diagrams to map each step in a process.
    - Highlight bottlenecks, manual tasks, and decision points where automation could add value.
- **Why They Matter:** Process mapping provides a clear understanding of workflows, ensuring no critical steps are overlooked during automation planning.

95 Risk Assessment Models

SWOT Analysis for Automation
- **What It Is:** A strategic planning tool to assess the internal and external factors that could impact your automation project.
- **How It Works:**
    - Strengths: What internal advantages does automation bring? (e.g., reducing costs, improving accuracy.)
    - Weaknesses: What internal challenges could hinder success? (e.g., employee resistance.)
    - Opportunities: What external trends support automation? (e.g., rising labor costs, competitive pressure.)
    - Threats: What external risks could derail the project? (e.g., regulatory hurdles, economic shifts.)

- **Why It Matters:** SWOT analysis gives a balanced view of the automation landscape, helping you anticipate challenges and capitalize on strengths.

Failure Modes and Effects Analysis (FMEA)
- **What It Is:** A proactive risk management tool to identify potential points of failure in a process and evaluate their impact.

- **How It Works:**
    - List each step in the process and potential failure modes (e.g., "bot fails to handle exceptions").
    - Assign severity, occurrence, and detection ratings to each failure mode.
    - Calculate a Risk Priority Number (RPN) to prioritize issues.

- **Why It Matters:** FMEA ensures you address the most critical risks before implementation, minimizing disruptions.

96   Implementation and Scalability Frameworks

Pilot-to-Scale Framework
- **What It Is:** A step-by-step approach to testing automation on a small scale before rolling it out organization wide.

- **How It Works:**
    - Select a low-risk, high-impact process for the pilot.
    - Measure the results (time saved, errors reduced, cost savings).

- Refine the solution based on feedback and scale to other processes.
- **Why It Matters:** Starting small reduces risk and builds confidence among stakeholders.

Kaizen for Continuous Improvement
- **What It Is:** A Japanese methodology focused on incremental, continuous improvements to workflows.
- **How It Works:**
  - Post-automation, monitor performance regularly.
  - Identify small tweaks or additional automation opportunities to further optimize processes.
- **Why It Matters:** Automation isn't a one-time effort—Kaizen ensures ongoing value by encouraging constant refinement.

97 How These Frameworks Work Together

Each of these frameworks addresses a different phase of the automation lifecycle:
1. **Identifying Opportunities:** Use the Automation Potential Matrix and Process Mapping Methodologies to find processes ripe for automation.
2. **Calculating ROI:** Apply Payback Period, NPV, and Sensitivity Analysis to estimate the financial impact of automation.
3. **Managing Risks:** Leverage SWOT and FMEA to anticipate challenges and build mitigation strategies.

4. **Scaling Success:** Start with the Pilot-to-Scale Framework and adopt Kaizen principles to drive continuous improvement.

By combining these tools, you can create a robust, strategic approach to automation that maximizes ROI while minimizing risks. These frameworks aren't just theoretical—they're practical roadmaps for turning automation into a sustainable competitive advantage.

www.ingramcontent.com/pod-product-compliance
Lightning Source LLC
Chambersburg PA
CBHW071056240526
45469CB00006BD/2324